A SUNDAY AFTERNOON

WHEN MOMENTS FREEZE AND VERSES FLOW

SRESHTHA GANGULY

Made with ❤ on the Notion Press Platform
www.notionpress.com

To my mother, for whose love, support, and countless sacrifices have shaped me into who I am today. And to the Almighty Power, for everything—Your guidance, grace, and blessings are woven through every word.

Contents

Contents

Preface

"A Sunday Afternoon" is a collection born out of stillness, reflection, and a desire to capture the fleeting moments that make up our lives. One Sunday afternoon, with the world moving slowly around me, I decided to write. There was no grand plan, no particular theme in mind—just a quiet yearning to leave something behind that might touch the hearts of others. In these pages, you'll find poems that speak to nostalgia, peacefulness, longing, and love. There are moments of melancholy, sadness, and a quiet thoughtfulness that echoes through every verse. These are the emotions that arise when we sit with our own thoughts, when we pause and listen to the beating of our hearts.

This book is not a polished work of perfection, but a collection of raw moments, feelings, and reflections. Each poem is a fragment of a larger story—the story of our shared human experience. They come from the depths of my own heart, yet I hope they speak to yours, too. For in our joy, sorrow, and everything in between, we are all connected. May these words remind you of your own quiet afternoons, your own moments of introspection, and the emotions that make us who we are. This is my humble offering to the world, a collection of poems meant to be felt, not just read.

Romantic and Divine Love

This section starts with the most direct and passionate expressions of love, from the magnetic pull of a soulmate to the intimacy and sacredness of physical connection.

1. Magnetic North

You are my magnetic north, my guiding star,
In every storm, no matter how far.
The world may spin, the compass may sway,
But your pull draws me, night and day.
Like a needle's fix, unwavering, true,
I follow your call, no matter what I do.
A silent force that pulls me near,
The only direction I hold dear.
Though skies may darken, winds may shift,
Your love is the gift, the sacred lift.
Magnetic north, in your arms I find,
A love eternal, by fate designed.

2. A Medieval Love

In castles high, beneath the sky,
Two souls in silence dared to fly.
A noble knight, with sword in hand,
A lady's heart, like golden sand.
Through winds that howl and storms that rise,
They shared soft glances, starry eyes.
No words could speak what hearts could feel,
A love so deep, a fate so real.
The moonlit paths, the gardens wide,
They walked as one, with love as guide.
In secret vows and tender smiles,
Their love endured through endless miles.
Their souls were bound, their fates aligned,
A medieval love, eternal, kind.

3. Forbidden Garden

In the garden where the moonlight falls,
A secret blooms, and temptation calls,
The air is thick with sweet, soft fear,
As innocence begins to disappear.
The touch of skin, the brush of lips,
The trembling hands, the stolen grips,
Chastity fades like morning mist,
As longing stirs in a lover's kiss.
The soil, now warm with love's embrace,
No turning back from this sacred place,
Two souls entwined, a fleeting dream,
In the garden's grasp, they softly scream.
With trembling hands, the gates we part,
As passion stirs the waiting heart,
The bloom of innocence is gone,
Yet in its loss, we both belong.

4. Your Body is a Roadway to Heaven

Your body is a roadway to heaven,
Where every touch feels like a blessing given.
Each curve, each line, a path so true,
Leading my heart straight back to you.
Your eyes, a doorway to sacred skies,
Where stars are born and time flies by.
Your lips, a promise I long to keep,
A journey to places where angels sleep.
With every step, your soul I trace,
In your embrace, I find my place.
Your body, my love, is heaven's door,
And I'll walk it with you, forevermore.

5. Only the Poets Know How to Love

Only the poets know how to love,
In whispers soft, like stars above.
They speak in verses, pure and deep,
Where shadows wake and angels sleep.
They write of hearts that burn and break,
Of endless rivers, still awake.
In every line, they breathe and sigh,
A love that cannot ask nor try.
Not bound by time, nor bound by space,
They find the truth in each embrace.
For only poets understand,
Love's language flows from heart to hand.

Longing, Regret, and Lost Love

These poems reflect on love lost, missed opportunities, and deep, lingering regrets, offering a bittersweet sense of longing. This section is emotional and reflective.

6. You Read My Poems No More

You read my poems no more,
So I write what I did before.
No need to hide or second-guess,
I spill my thoughts with no distress.
The pages fill, my heart takes flight,
You won't see the words I write.
Each verse a secret, kept from you,
A quiet space where dreams are true.
You won't know what lies behind,
The silent thoughts I leave unsigned.
I write for me, for what I feel,
A world inside, so pure, so real.

7. I Wish You Lasted till Summer

I wish you lasted till summer's light,
When days grow long, and hearts take flight.
When flowers bloom and skies turn blue,
I long for one more day with you.
The cold winds came, too soon, too fast,
And left us with a love that couldn't last.
Your warmth, a fire in winter's chill,
Now fades away, against my will.
I dream of sunsets, golden and sweet,
Where we could walk on sun-kissed streets.
But time was cruel, it stole you away,
Before we reached that summer day.
I would have held you through the dawn,
While seasons turned, and light was born.
I would have watched the world unfold,
With you beside me, strong and bold.
Yet now I hold your memory near,
A quiet ache that won't disappear.
I wish you lasted through the sun,
But now I wait for warmth to come.
In the quiet moments, I'll still hear,
The echo of your voice so clear—

A whispered wish upon the breeze:
"I wish you lasted till summer's ease."

8. If I Knew It was Our Last Kiss

If I knew it was our last kiss,

I'd kiss you all night, in timeless bliss.

Every touch would linger, slow and deep,

A promise in silence, one I'd keep.

Your lips, like whispers, soft and sweet,

Would hold the world, make time retreat.

I'd savor the warmth of your embrace,

The memory of you, the look on your face.

No words needed, just hearts aligned,

In that kiss, our souls entwined.

If I knew it was our last goodbye,

I'd kiss you forever, under the sky.

9. The Mistake I Never Regret

You're the mistake I didn't regret making,

A risk I took, with my heart wide awake in.

A wrong that felt like something pure,

A wild hope I couldn't ignore.

Through tangled words and silent nights,

You were the spark in darkened sights.

I wandered lost, yet found my place,

In every flaw, I saw your grace.

You're the choice I'll always own,

A love in chaos, brightly grown.

And though it's gone, the truth I'll keep—

You're the mistake I still don't regret to keep.

Through chaos, laughter, love, and pain,

You were the sun that broke the rain.

No map to guide, no way to see,

Yet, I'm glad you wandered close to me.

A wrong that felt so right inside,

A storm I chose to ride,

Though we may part, I won't forget—

You're the mistake I never regret.

10. Ode to the One I Left Behind

Oh, love, to you, I write this song,

For though I've gone, I've not gone long.

Your touch, still burns within my veins,

A whisper lost in distant plains.

I left, unsure of where to roam,

But in my chest, you are my home.

The roads I walk may lead me far,

But you remain my northern star.

The moonlight falls, and in its glow,

I see your face in all I know—

In every breeze, in every sigh,

In whispered winds, I hear you cry.

I never meant to turn away,

But time, it calls, and I must stray.

Yet, in the stillness of the night,

I dream of you, of holding tight.

I left you, love, to chase a light,

But none so bright as what was right—

Your heart, the rhythm of my soul,

The only truth that makes me whole.

The world may change, and seasons bend,

But you, my love, you are the end—

The place I'll rest when all is done,
The warmth, the fire, the setting sun.
So though I roam, my heart remains
Entwined with yours, through joys and pains.
I left, but only for a time—
Your love will always be my rhyme.

Transformation through Love, Loss, and Time

Poems in this section deal with the transformation that comes through experiencing love, loss, and change over time. The imagery is poignant and speaks to healing, resilience, and the wisdom gained through life's challenges.

11. Chronicles of the Forgotten Warriors

In the shadows where silence weeps,

Lie tales of warriors, whose honor sleeps,

Their names lost in the winds of time,

Echoes now fading, like a distant rhyme.

They fought on fields where the earth was stained,

With blood that soaked and hearts that pained,

Yet none recall their fierce, bold cries,

For history's pages, their names deny.

Their swords were sharp, their hearts were strong,

They marched as one, a thunderous song,

But in the end, the world moved on,

And their story vanished with the dawn.

No statues rise, no banners fly,

No songs to sing, no tearful sigh,

But in the quiet, if you listen near,

You'll hear their whispers, faint but clear.

They are the ones who never died,

Whose spirit lives on, undenied,

In every storm, in every fight,

In every heart that knows the night.

So let us remember, though unseen,

The forgotten warriors who've always been,

For in the dust of ages past,
Their legacy will forever last.

12. Butterfly with Broken Wings

A butterfly, once bright and bold,

Flutters now with wings of gold,

But something's wrong, it cannot fly,

It dreams of soaring through the sky.

The winds are soft, the skies are wide,

Yet it can only crawl, not glide.

A fracture deep, a silent tear,

Has stilled the grace that once was there.

Its wings, once painted in the sun,

Now hang in silence, undone.

But still, it tries, though weak and frail,

A heart that hopes despite the hail.

For in the dust, there lies a song,

A quiet strength, where it belongs.

Though wings are torn and shadows fall,

It rises up—still standing tall.

The broken wings, though bruised and scarred,

Carry the beauty of a soul unmarred.

A fragile flight that dares to sing,

The butterfly with broken wings.

13. Sweet Tragedies

I find beauty in sweet tragedies,
Where sorrow weaves through soft melodies.
In broken hearts that softly sigh,
Like sunset colors in the sky.
The quiet ache that love will bring,
A fleeting joy, a whispered sting.
In every tear that falls like rain,
There's something pure, a subtle gain.
For in the cracks, the light can shine,
And flaws make moments so divine.
Through pain, I see what life can be,
A dance of joy and mystery.
I find beauty in sweet tragedies,
Where love and loss are intertwined, free.

14. Remnants of a Festival

Remnants of a festival, scattered in the breeze,
Faded ribbons caught in the limbs of the trees.
Whispers of laughter, now soft and far,
Lingering like traces of a distant star.
The ground still hums with the joy we shared,
Echoes of songs once sung, now pared.
Tattered flags flutter where colors once bloomed,
Ghosts of the dancers who once filled the room.
Candles burned low, their light now dim,
Like memories fading at the edge of a hymn.
Time has unraveled what we held so dear,
Yet the heart still yearns, though the end is near.

15. I Painted You in My Poetry

I painted you in my poetry,
With strokes of light, soft hues,
Each line a whispered memory,
A canvas born from you.
Your laughter colored every rhyme,
Your touch, a quiet shade,
And in the quiet folds of time,
Your presence gently laid.
I mixed the shades of morning skies,
With echoes of your voice,
Each verse a moment's sweet surprise,
Where words became our choice.
In every stanza, I could see,
The shape of you, divine—
Your spirit etched in every plea,
A brushstroke of the mind.
I painted you in ink and air,
In every word, you bled,
A masterpiece beyond compare,
In places words had tread.
Though ink may fade and verses end,
Your image still will stay—

A portrait in my heart, my friend,
Forever on display.

Self-Discovery, Growth, and Reflection

The focus here shifts from romantic love to personal growth, self-reflection, and the process of understanding oneself. These poems explore the journey both within and outside, showing how choices shape us.

16. You are "My Road Not Taken"

You, the road not taken, wide and steep,

A silent path where secrets sleep.

I glance and wonder where you'd lead,

A whispered call, a distant need.

But here I stand, with choices made,

And in my heart, your echoes fade.

You linger still, a haunting song,

The road I never walked along.

17. My Favorite Incomplete Wish

A wish that lingers, half-untold,
A fleeting dream, a secret goal.
It sits upon my heart's own shelf,
Unfinished, like a book itself.
The ending waits, a whispered plea,
But life moves on so restlessly.
My favorite wish, it dances near,
A perfect hope, yet never clear.

18. The Journey of Getting Somewhere

The road unwinds, a steady pace,
With every turn, a new embrace.
The sunlight dances on the stream,
The quiet hum of life's soft dream.
Footsteps echo on the earth,
Each one a mark of joy and worth.
The scent of pine, the song of rain,
The touch of winds that ease the strain.
No rush to reach, no end to seek,
In every pause, the soul feels weak.
For in the journey, day by day,
We find our hearts along the way.

19. I'm in Love with Odd Things

I'm in love with odd things,
The crooked smile that morning brings.
The quiet hum of an old street light,
The way the moon spills through the night.
I love the cracks in fading walls,
The sound of rain on empty halls.
The scent of books that time has kissed,
The way the sun fades in the mist.
I find my joy in what's misplaced,
In beauty born of time and space.
For in these oddities, I see
The perfect truth that sets me free.

20. Growing Old is a Gift

Growing old is a gift, a treasure to find,

With each wrinkle a story, a memory to bind.

The years softly whisper of lessons we've learned,

Of bridges we've crossed, and how we have yearned.

The silver of hair, the wisdom of eyes,

The peace that comes when we no longer disguise.

Each laugh, each tear, a moment that stays,

A tapestry woven through the passage of days.

Though time may slow and the body may bend,

The heart grows stronger, it's not the end.

For growing old is a journey, not fear,

A gift we unwrap as we draw near.

Mysticism, Nature, and Eternal Truths

This section delves into themes of nature, spirituality, and the mystical forces that shape human experience. These poems evoke a sense of the eternal, of something greater than oneself, blending the natural world with deeper truths.

21. Guardians of the Enchanted Scrolls

In hidden realms, where shadows fold,
Lie ancient tomes of secrets told.
The scrolls, with whispers soft and deep,
Guard truths that dreamers long to keep.
With ink that glows like moonlit streams,
And parchment woven from lost dreams,
The guardians stand, a silent might,
Protecting knowledge veiled in light.
Their eyes are stars, their hearts are fire,
They stand to quell the dark desire,
That seeks to steal the magic grand,
Of ancient words, in mystic hands.
Through storms and years, through time they wait,
To guard the scrolls from twisted fate.
Their voices speak in riddles clear,
To guide the chosen, hearts sincere.
With every turn, the scrolls unbind,
Revealing secrets of the mind—
The guardians' oath is sworn in gold,
To shield the truths the scrolls behold.
So if you seek what none may know,
Beware the path that winds below,

For only those with heart and soul,
Can face the trials of the enchanted scroll.

22. Song of a Thousand Druids

Beneath the ancient, whispering trees,

Where moonlight dances on the breeze,

A thousand voices, soft and deep,

Awake from centuries of sleep.

They call to earth, to sky, to sea,

To winds that roam eternally.

Their song begins, a sacred thread,

Woven in the heart of dead.

With hands that touch the roots of time,

They sing in rhythm, pure, sublime.

The stones remember, and the stars,

Echoing tales from ancient scars.

The rivers hum a mournful tune,

While shadows dance beneath the moon.

The fire flickers, golden bright,

As druids chant through endless night.

Their voices rise and fall like tides,

In harmony where magic hides.

They speak the language of the trees,

And hear the songs of distant seas.

A thousand druids, one with earth,

Their wisdom old, of boundless worth.

Through the veil of mist they weave,
A world where time itself believes.
And in the silence that remains,
A single voice, with power, reigns—
A melody that never dies,
A song beneath the endless skies.

23. Return of the Lost Angels

Beneath the silent, mourning skies,
A thousand wings begin to rise,
From shadows deep, where they were cast,
The lost angels come at last.
They wandered far in distant dreams,
Where silver rivers meet moonbeams,
Their voices lost in winds that weep,
Now they awaken from their sleep.
Their eyes are mirrors, bright and pure,
Reflecting all that must endure—
The scars of time, the weight of sin,
Yet they return with hearts within.
Through broken clouds, they softly glide,
A chorus rising with the tide,
Of prayers unspoken, hopes unseen,
They bring the light where dark has been.
Their wings are woven from the sky,
Of comet tails and dreams that fly,
And as they touch the earth once more,
They heal the hearts, restore the sore.
For every soul they seek to mend,
A broken path will find its end.

The lost angels, with love untold,
Return to warm the hearts gone cold.
In quiet grace, they stand once more,
By every shore, at every door,
And in their wake, the world will know—
The lost angels are here to show.
That even in the darkest night,
There's always hope, there's always light.
So let them guide, let them ascend—
The lost angels, now our friends.

24. Dawn of Sacred Truths

The night retreats, its shadows thin,
As dawn awakes, a light within.
A whispered breath, a stirring breeze,
The sacred truths that time conceives.
Beneath the sky's first tender hue,
The world reveals its heart anew,
As if the earth, with quiet grace,
Unveils the secrets of its face.
The sun, a flame of endless fire,
Ignites the soul's most deep desire,
To see the world through clearer eyes,
And hear the song of ancient skies.
Each dawn is but a fleeting prayer,
A moment born of light and air,
Where every truth is softly known,
A sacred gift to call our own.
In every ray, in every sound,
The wisdom of the world is found,
Not in the stars or in the sky,
But in the silence we pass by.
The dawn, it speaks of things unseen,
Of life beyond the in-between,

Of love that swells with quiet might,
And all the truths that come with light.
So as the sun climbs ever high,
We listen, watch, and wonder why—
For in each dawn, a truth unspoken,
A sacred world remains unbroken.

25. A Walk down the Poetry Alley

A walk down the poetry alley,
Where shadows hum and dreamers rally,
Each step a verse, each breath a rhyme,
Unfolding stories lost in time.
The cobblestones whisper in soft refrain,
Echoes of joy, echoes of pain.
Beneath the arches, words take flight,
Flickering like stars in the velvet night.
The air is thick with untold dreams,
Of silent poets and moonlit streams.
In the alley, where the muses dwell,
Every heart finds a tale to tell.

Notes

Forbidden Garden

The poem portrays the journey from innocence to intimacy within the metaphor of a "forbidden garden." It highlights the feelings of nervousness, desire, and inevitability that accompany the loss of purity. The garden represents a private, sacred space where this transformation takes place, and the experience is both powerful and irreversible. The "gates" represent the transition from innocence to experience, and the "trembling hands" suggest hesitation or nervousness as they open this new chapter together. Ultimately, the loss of innocence is not depicted as tragic but as a path to deeper connection and belonging.

Notes

Butterfly with Broken Wings

The poem celebrates the idea that brokenness doesn't erase value or beauty. The butterfly, despite its broken wings, still embodies grace, resilience, and hope.

Notes

My Favorite Incomplete Wish

The poem reflects a feeling of yearning for something that seems important but hasn't materialized yet—an incomplete wish that holds both beauty and frustration. "A perfect hope, yet never clear": The wish is ideal in the speaker's mind but remains uncertain, elusive, and hard to define.

Notes

Guardians of the Enchanted Scrolls

The guardians are not only protectors but also guides. Their "riddles" and their guidance help those with good intentions to navigate the path toward knowledge, ensuring that the power within the scrolls does not fall into the wrong hands. Overall, the poem reflects the themes of wisdom, protection, responsibility, and the balance between light and dark forces in the pursuit of knowledge.

Notes

Song of a Thousand Druids

The poem is an invocation of ancient wisdom, showing the druids as spiritual beings deeply attuned to nature's cycles and mysteries. Their song is a ritual that connects all elements of existence—earth, sky, sea, and time itself. The druids act as intermediaries between the physical and spiritual worlds, invoking a deep, primal magic that transcends generations. The poem also suggests that this wisdom is timeless, influencing the natural world in subtle but profound ways.

Notes

Return of the Lost Angels

The poem is about the return of something beautiful and transformative—whether it's love, guidance, or hope—that has been absent for a time but now returns to heal and guide. The "lost angels" represent these forces of light and healing that help restore what was broken, offering a new beginning for those in need.

Notes

Dawn of Sacred Truths

Unbroken Sacredness: The concluding idea is that these sacred truths, like the rising sun, are constant and eternal. They are not broken or fleeting but always available to those who seek them, suggesting that understanding and wisdom are perennial forces in life. In essence, the poem highlights how every day, like the dawn, holds potential for spiritual insight, urging us to be mindful and attuned to the deeper layers of reality that often go unnoticed.

Biography

Sreshtha Ganguly is a poet, writer, and scholar from Kolkata. With an MSc in Chemistry (2021) and currently pursuing her PhD at Indian Institute of Technology Kharagpur, she is driven by a deep curiosity for both the sciences and the arts. From an early age, Sreshtha has been enchanted by the power of words, particularly those that rhyme and resonate with the heart. Beyond her academic pursuits, she enjoys reading, traveling, and finding inspiration in the world around her. Through poetry, she seeks to feed her soul and create something truly meaningful—something big, something that the world will remember her for. With a passion for blending intellect and imagination, Sreshtha dreams of leaving a lasting legacy through both her writing and her contributions to the world.

Follow her poetic journey on Instagram: @_thepassengerprincess